good NEWS BIBLE

Paul's letter to the

ROMANS

AF477061

Bible Society
Trinity Business Centre
Stonehill Green, Westlea
Swindon SN5 7DG
biblesociety.org.uk

Copyright © 2017 The British and Foreign Bible Society(BFBS)
Map produced for BFBS by Hardlines © 1997, Revised by BFBS 2017
Additional material © 2017 BFBS

Good News Translation® (Today's English Version, Second Edition)
© 1992 American Bible Society. All rights reserved.
Anglicisation © The British and Foreign Bible Society 1976, 1994,
2004

The copyright for the derivative work of Anglicisation pertains
only to the text within the Good News Translation (GNT) that
British and Foreign Bible Society adapted for British literary usage,
consistent with Section 103(b) of the United States Copyright Act,
17 U.S.C. § 103(b).

Bible text from the Good News Translation (GNT) is not to be
reproduced in copies or otherwise by any means except as
permitted in writing by American Bible Society, 101 North
Independence Mall East, Floor 8, Philadelphia, PA 19106-2155
(www.americanbible.org).

All rights reserved. No part of this publication may be reproduced
or transmitted in any form or by any means, electronic or
mechanical, including photocopy, recording or any information
storage or retrieval system, without permission in writing from the
publisher.

Paul's letter to the Romans
ISBN: 978-0-564-05137-3
Typesetting and production management by Bible Society
Resources Ltd, a wholly-owned subsidiary of The British and
Foreign Bible Society

Cover design by Colin Hall

BSRL/2017/1.55M
Printed in Great Britain

Contents

Welcome to the Good News Bible

Welcome to this dyslexia-friendly edition of Paul's letter to the Romans, using text from the Good News Bible.

If you are dyslexic, you may find most Bibles very difficult to read, with their small type, long paragraphs and thin paper. This book has been specially designed with the British Dyslexia Association's style guide in mind, so it has the following features:

- Thicker paper, so that type does not show through

- Cream-coloured paper

- Matt paper

- Plain font

- Larger type

- Wider line spacing

- Short paragraphs

- Bold headings

The Good News Bible is a clear, easy-to read translation of the Bible. It uses ordinary, everyday language so that as many people as possible can read and understand it. This has made it a very popular translation, selling over 150 million copies in the UK alone.

About the Bible

The Bible isn't one book but a collection of books, one of them being Paul's letter to the Romans. These books were written at different times by different people. They include many types of writing, such as history, poetry, stories, laws, letters, visions, songs and prayers.

The Bible has two main sections, known as the Old Testament and the New Testament. The Old Testament contains the story of God's relationship with the Israelites, over hundreds of years. It was written mainly in the Hebrew language, with some parts in a language called Aramaic.

The New Testament continues the story. It tells us about Jesus Christ and how his first followers began to spread the Christian message across the world. It was written in Greek, a language spoken through most of the Roman empire.

Even the newest parts of the Bible are about 2,000 years old, and many parts are much older. This means that everyone who reads it today will find some parts of it hard to understand. It might be helpful if you try to imagine what life was like for the people who first read it. Then think about what the words might mean for us today.

If you focus on the parts you do understand, not the parts you find difficult, there will always be something interesting to learn.

Finding your way around Paul's letter to the Romans

Most of the books in the New Testament are actually letters. Some are written to individuals and some to whole churches, aiming to encourage the first Christian believers in their faith.

Paul's letter to the Romans is the longest of them and is quite complicated. Paul was one of the most important early Christian leaders. In this letter, he explains why people need to be saved from their sins, and how they can find that salvation through faith in Jesus Christ.

If you're reading the letter to the Romans on your own, it's a good idea to read it from beginning to end. This will give you an idea of how Paul's beliefs about faith and salvation fit together. However, if you are in church or at a study group, someone might ask you to look up the reference for a verse or short passage.

References are always given in this order – book title, chapter title and verse number. For example, Romans 5.6 means the fifth chapter of Romans, and the sixth verse of that chapter.

In this book, the chapter numbers are in very large type on a separate line. The verse numbers are the very small numbers that you can see as you read the story.

You can also follow the chapter and verse numbers through the book by looking at the reference at the top of each page.

Enjoy reading!

It is all too easy to assume that we know exactly what a Bible story says, especially if it's a famous one or we have heard it many times before. If this book helps you to read Romans for yourself more easily, you might find that you understand it in a new way.

Don't be afraid to ask questions about what you are reading. What excites you? What confuses you? Which are your favourite verses or stories? Write notes for yourself, or draw pictures, or memorise the words so that you can think further about them later.

Why not get together with other people to read Paul's letter to the Romans? We all bring our own experiences and thoughts to the Bible, so it can be helpful to talk about it together and find out how other people understand it.

If you've enjoyed this book, the Gospel of Mark, the Gospel of John and the book of Psalms are also available in a dyslexia-friendly version. Go to our website, biblesociety.org.uk, to find out more.

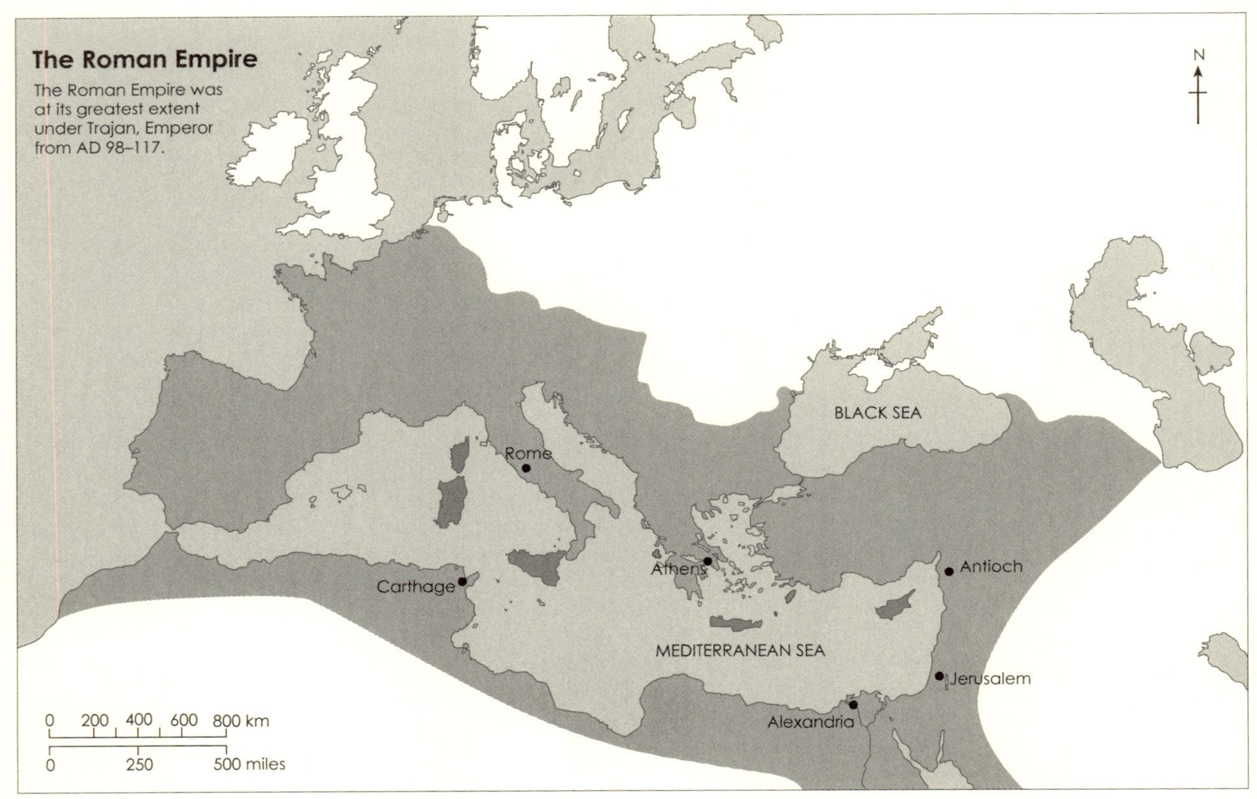

The Roman Empire
The Roman Empire was at its greatest extent under Trajan, Emperor from AD 98–117.
N
BLACK SEA
MEDITERRANEAN SEA
Rome
Carthage
Athens
Antioch
Jerusalem
Alexandria
0 200 400 600 800 km
0 250 500 miles

Paul's letter to the Romans

The letter of the covenant

What's it about? The letter was probably written because the church in Rome had some problems – in particular, tension between Jews and Gentiles (non-Jews). The letter explains how the old covenant (obeying the Law of Moses) connects with the new covenant (believing in Jesus Christ).

Who wrote it? Paul was a Pharisee who persecuted the followers of Jesus. However, after a dramatic meeting with Jesus, Paul became a missionary for him. He travelled around the Roman empire, starting churches and writing to encourage Christians everywhere. This is his letter to the church in Rome, written around AD 57.

Why read it? The letter to the Romans is an explanation of faith in Jesus, taking in God's judgement and the salvation that can be found in Jesus.

What's special about it? Romans is the only letter in which we read of Paul's hopes for the salvation of Jews and Gentiles together. In the last chapter, he sends warm greetings to a long list of his friends and fellow workers in the church, both men and women. Many of these names are found nowhere else in the New Testament.

Chapter 1

1 From Paul, a servant of Christ Jesus and an apostle chosen and called by God to preach his Good News.

2 The Good News was promised long ago by God through his prophets, as written in the Holy Scriptures.

3 It is about his Son, our Lord Jesus Christ: as to his humanity, he was born a descendant of David; 4 as to his divine holiness, he was shown with great power to be the Son of God by being raised from death.

5 Through him God gave me the privilege of being an apostle for the sake of Christ, in order to lead people of all nations to believe and obey.

6 This also includes you who are in Rome, whom God has called to belong to Jesus Christ.

7 And so I write to all of you in Rome whom God loves and has called to be his own people:

May God our Father and the Lord Jesus Christ give you grace and peace.

Prayer of Thanksgiving

8 First, I thank my God through Jesus Christ for all of you, because the whole world is hearing about your faith.

9 God is my witness that what I say is true — the God whom I serve with all my heart by preaching the Good News about his Son. God knows that I remember you 10 every time I pray. I ask that God in his good will may at last make it possible for me to visit you now.

11 For I want very much to see you, in order to share a spiritual blessing with you to make you strong.

12 What I mean is that both you and I will be helped at the same time, you by my faith and I by yours.

13 You must remember, my brothers and sisters, that many times I have planned to visit you, but something has always kept me from doing so. I want to win converts among you also, as I have among other Gentiles.

14 For I have an obligation to all peoples, to the civilized and to the savage, to the educated and to the ignorant.

15 So then, I am eager to preach the Good News to you also who live in Rome.

The Power of the Gospel

16 I have complete confidence in the gospel; it is God's power to save all who believe, first the Jews and also the Gentiles.

17 For the gospel reveals how God puts people right with himself: it is through faith from beginning to end. As

the scripture says, "The person who is put right with God through faith shall live."**a**

The Guilt of the Human Race

18 God's anger is revealed from heaven against all the sin and evil of the people whose evil ways prevent the truth from being known.

19 God punishes them, because what can be known about God is plain to them, for God himself made it plain.

20 Ever since God created the world, his invisible qualities, both his eternal power and his divine nature, have been clearly seen; they are perceived in the things that God has made. So those people have no excuse at all!

21 They know God, but they do not give him the honour that belongs to him, nor do they thank him. Instead, their thoughts have become complete nonsense, and their empty minds are filled with darkness.

22 They say they are wise, but they are fools; 23 instead of worshipping the immortal God, they worship images made to look like mortal human beings or birds or animals or reptiles.

24 And so God has given those people over to do the filthy things their hearts desire, and they do shameful things with each other.

---

a *put right with God through faith shall live; or put right with God shall live through faith.*

"Instead of worshipping ... God, they worship images" (1.23)

25 They exchange the truth about God for a lie; they worship and serve what God has created instead of the Creator himself, who is to be praised for ever! Amen.

26 Because they do this, God has given them over to shameful passions. Even the women pervert the natural use of their sex by unnatural acts.

27 In the same way the men give up natural sexual relations with women and burn with passion for each other. Men do shameful things with each other, and as a result they bring upon themselves the punishment they deserve for their wrongdoing.

28 Because those people refuse to keep in mind the true knowledge about God, he has given them over to corrupted minds, so that they do the things that they should not do.

29 They are filled with all kinds of wickedness, evil, greed, and vice; they are full of jealousy, murder, fighting, deceit,

and malice. They gossip [30] and speak evil of one another; they are hateful to God, insolent,*b* proud, and boastful; they think of more ways to do evil; they disobey their parents; [31] they have no conscience; they do not keep their promises, and they show no kindness or pity for others.

[32] They know that God's law says that people who live in this way deserve death. Yet, not only do they continue to do these very things, but they even approve of others who do them.

Chapter 2

God's Judgement

[1] Do you, my friend, pass judgement on others? You have no excuse at all, whoever you are. For when you judge others and then do the same things which they do, you condemn yourself.

[2] We know that God is right when he judges the people who do such things as these.

[3] But you, my friend, do those very things for which you pass judgement on others! Do you think you will escape God's judgement?

[4] Or perhaps you despise his great kindness, tolerance, and patience. Surely you know that God is kind, because he is trying to lead you to repent.

---

b *are hateful to God, insolent; or hate God, and are insolent.*

5 But you have a hard and stubborn heart, and so you are making your own punishment even greater on the Day when God's anger and righteous judgements will be revealed.

6 For God will reward every person according to what each has done.

7 Some people keep on doing good, and seek glory, honour, and immortal life; to them God will give eternal life.

8 Other people are selfish and reject what is right, in order to follow what is wrong; on them God will pour out his anger and fury.

9 There will be suffering and pain for all those who do what is evil, for the Jews first and also for the Gentiles.

10 But God will give glory, honour, and peace to all who do what is good, to the Jews first and also to the Gentiles.

11 For God judges everyone by the same standard.

12 The Gentiles do not have the Law of Moses; they sin and are lost apart from the Law. The Jews have the Law; they sin and are judged by the Law.

13 For it is not by hearing the Law that people are put right with God, but by doing what the Law commands.

14 The Gentiles do not have the Law; but whenever they do by instinct what the Law commands, they are their own law, even though they do not have the Law.

15 Their conduct shows that what the Law commands is written in their hearts. Their consciences also show that this

is true, since their thoughts sometimes accuse them and sometimes defend them.

16 And so, according to the Good News I preach, this is how it will be on that Day when God through Jesus Christ will judge the secret thoughts of all.

The Jews and the Law

17 What about you? You call yourself a Jew; you depend on the Law and boast about God; 18 you know what God wants you to do, and you have learnt from the Law to choose what is right; 19 you are sure that you are a guide for the blind, a light for those who are in darkness, 20 an instructor for the foolish, and a teacher for the ignorant. You are certain that in the Law you have the full content of knowledge and of truth.

21 You teach others — why don't you teach yourself? You preach, "Do not steal" — but do you yourself steal?

22 You say, "Do not commit adultery" — but do you commit adultery? You detest idols — but do you rob temples?

23 You boast about having God's law — but do you bring shame on God by breaking his law?

24 The scripture says, "Because of you Jews, the Gentiles speak evil of God."

25 If you obey the Law, your circumcision is of value; but if you disobey the Law, you might as well never have been circumcised.

26 If the Gentile, who is not circumcised, obeys the commands of the Law, will God not regard him as though he were circumcised?

27 And so you Jews will be condemned by the Gentiles because you break the Law, even though you have it written down and are circumcised; but they obey the Law, even though they are not physically circumcised.

28 After all, who is a real Jew, truly circumcised? It is not the man who is a Jew on the outside, whose circumcision is a physical thing.

29 Rather, the real Jew is the person who is a Jew on the inside, that is, whose heart has been circumcised, and this is the work of God's Spirit, not of the written Law. Such a person receives praise from God, not from human beings.

Chapter 3

1 Have the Jews then any advantage over the Gentiles? Or is there any value in being circumcised?

2 Much, indeed, in every way! In the first place, God trusted his message to the Jews.

3 But what if some of them were not faithful? Does this mean that God will not be faithful?

4 Certainly not! God must be true, even though every human being is a liar. As the scripture says,

"You must be shown to be right when you speak;
you must win your case when you are being
tried."

5 But what if our doing wrong serves to show up more clearly God's doing right? Can we say that God does wrong when he punishes us? (This would be the natural question to ask.) 6 By no means! If God is not just, how can he judge the world?

7 But what if my untruth serves God's glory by making his truth stand out more clearly? Why should I still be condemned as a sinner?

8 Why not say, then, "Let us do evil so that good may come"? Some people, indeed, have insulted me by accusing me of saying this very thing! They will be condemned, as they should be.

No one is Righteous

9 Well then, are we Jews in any better condition than the Gentiles? Not at all!c I have already shown that Jews and Gentiles alike are all under the power of sin.

10 As the Scriptures say:

"There is no one who is righteous,
11no one who is wise
or who worships God.

---

c *any better condition than the Gentiles? Not at all!; or any worse condition than the Gentiles? Not altogether.*

12All have turned away from God;
they have all gone wrong;
no one does what is right, not even one.
13Their words are full of deadly deceit;
wicked lies roll off their tongues,
and dangerous threats, like snake's poison, from
their lips;
14their speech is filled with bitter curses.
15They are quick to hurt and kill;
16they leave ruin and destruction wherever they go.
17They have not known the path of peace,
18nor have they learnt reverence for God."

19Now we know that everything in the Law applies to those who live under the Law, in order to stop all human excuses and bring the whole world under God's judgement.

20For no one is put right in God's sight by doing what the Law requires; what the Law does is to make people know that they have sinned.

How We are Put Right with God

21But now God's way of putting people right with himself has been revealed. It has nothing to do with law, even though the Law of Moses and the prophets gave their witness to it.

22God puts people right through their faith in Jesus Christ. God does this to all who believe in Christ, because there is no difference at all: 23 everyone has sinned and is far away from God's saving presence.

24 But by the free gift of God's grace all are put right with him through Christ Jesus, who sets them free.

25-26 God offered him, so that by his blood**d** he should become the means by which people's sins are forgiven through their faith in him. God did this in order to demonstrate that he is righteous. In the past he was patient and overlooked people's sins; but in the present time he deals with their sins, in order to demonstrate his righteousness. In this way God shows that he himself is righteous and that he puts right everyone who believes in Jesus.

27 What, then, can we boast about? Nothing! And what is the reason for this? Is it that we obey the Law? No, but that we believe.

28 For we conclude that a person is put right with God only through faith, and not by doing what the Law commands.

29 Or is God the God of the Jews only? Is he not the God of the Gentiles also? Of course he is.

30 God is one, and he will put the Jews right with himself on the basis of their faith, and will put the Gentiles right through their faith.

31 Does this mean that by this faith we do away with the Law? No, not at all; instead, we uphold the Law.

---

d *by his blood; or by his sacrificial death.*

Chapter 4

The Example of Abraham

¹ What shall we say, then, of Abraham, the father of our race? What was his experience?

² If he was put right with God by the things he did, he would have something to boast about — but not in God's sight.

³ The scripture says, "Abraham believed God, and because of his faith God accepted him as righteous."

⁴ Those who work are paid wages, but they are not regarded as a gift; they are something that has been earned.

⁵ But those who depend on faith, not on deeds, and who believe in the God who declares the guilty to be innocent, it is this faith that God takes into account in order to put them right with himself.

⁶ This is what David meant when he spoke of the happiness of the person whom God accepts as righteous, apart from anything that person does:

⁷ "Happy are those whose wrongs are forgiven,
　　whose sins are pardoned!
⁸ Happy is the person whose sins the Lord will not keep
　　account of!"

⁹ Does this happiness that David spoke of belong only to those who are circumcised? No indeed! It belongs also to those who are not circumcised. For we have quoted the scripture, "Abraham believed God, and because of his faith God accepted him as righteous."

10 When did this take place? Was it before or after Abraham was circumcised? It was before, not after.

11 He was circumcised later, and his circumcision was a sign to show that because of his faith God had accepted him as righteous before he had been circumcised. And so Abraham is the spiritual father of all who believe in God and are accepted as righteous by him, even though they are not circumcised.

12 He is also the father of those who are circumcised, that is, of those who, in addition to being circumcised, also live the same life of faith that our father Abraham lived before he was circumcised.

God's Promise is Received through Faith

13 When God promised Abraham and his descendants that the world would belong to him, he did so, not because Abraham obeyed the Law, but because he believed and was accepted as righteous by God.

14 For if what God promises is to be given to those who obey the Law, then faith means nothing and God's promise is worthless.

15 The Law brings down God's anger; but where there is no law, there is no disobeying of the law.

16 And so the promise was based on faith, in order that the promise should be guaranteed as God's free gift to all of Abraham's descendants — not just to those who obey the Law, but also to those who believe as Abraham did. For Abraham is the spiritual father of us all; 17 as the scripture

says, "I have made you father of many nations." So the promise is good in the sight of God, in whom Abraham believed — the God who brings the dead to life and whose command brings into being what did not exist.

18 Abraham believed and hoped, even when there was no reason for hoping, and so became "the father of many nations." Just as the scripture says, "Your descendants will be as many as the stars."

19 He was then almost 100 years old; but his faith did not weaken when he thought of his body, which was already practically dead, or of the fact that Sarah could not have children.

20 His faith did not leave him, and he did not doubt God's promise; his faith filled him with power, and he gave praise to God.

21 He was absolutely sure that God would be able to do what he had promised.

22 That is why Abraham, through faith, "was accepted as righteous by God".

23 The words "he was accepted as righteous" were not written for him alone.

24 They were written also for us who are to be accepted as righteous, who believe in him who raised Jesus our Lord from death.

25 Because of our sins he was handed over to die, and he was raised to life in order to put us right with God.

Chapter 5

Right with God

¹ Now that we have been put right with God through faith, we have[e] peace with God through our Lord Jesus Christ.

² He has brought us by faith into this experience of God's grace, in which we now live. And so we boast[f] of the hope we have of sharing God's glory!

³ We also boast[g] of our troubles, because we know that trouble produces endurance, ⁴ endurance brings God's approval, and his approval creates hope.

⁵ This hope does not disappoint us, for God has poured out his love into our hearts by means of the Holy Spirit, who is God's gift to us.

⁶ For when we were still helpless, Christ died for the wicked at the time that God chose.

⁷ It is a difficult thing for someone to die for a righteous person. It may even be that someone might dare to die for a good person.

⁸ But God has shown us how much he loves us — it was while we were still sinners that Christ died for us!

⁹ By his blood[h] we are now put right with God; how much more, then, will we be saved by him from God's anger!

---

e *we have*; some manuscripts have *let us have*.
f *we boast*; or *let us boast*.
g *We also boast*; or *Let us also boast*.
h *By his blood*; or *By his sacrificial death*.

10 We were God's enemies, but he made us his friends through the death of his Son. Now that we are God's friends, how much more will we be saved by Christ's life!

11 But that is not all; we rejoice because of what God has done through our Lord Jesus Christ, who has now made us God's friends.

Adam and Christ

12 Sin came into the world through one man, and his sin brought death with it. As a result, death has spread to the whole human race because everyone has sinned.

13 There was sin in the world before the Law was given; but where there is no law, no account is kept of sins.

14 But from the time of Adam to the time of Moses death ruled over the whole human race, even over those who did not sin in the same way that Adam did when he disobeyed God's command.

Adam was a figure of the one who was to come.

15 But the two are not the same, because God's free gift is not like Adam's sin. It Is true that many people died because of the sin of that one man. But God's grace is much greater, and so is his free gift to so many people through the grace of the one man, Jesus Christ.

16 And there is a difference between God's gift and the sin of one man. After the one sin, came the judgement of "Guilty"; but after so many sins, comes the undeserved gift of "Not guilty!"

17It is true that through the sin of one man death began to rule because of that one man. But how much greater is the result of what was done by the one man, Jesus Christ! All who receive God's abundant grace and are freely put right with him will rule in life through Christ.

18So then, as the one sin condemned all people, in the same way the one righteous act sets all people free and gives them life.

19And just as the mass of people were made sinners as the result of the disobedience of one man, in the same way the mass of people will all be put right with God as the result of the obedience of the one man.

20Law was introduced in order to increase wrongdoing; but where sin increased, God's grace increased much more.

21So then, just as sin ruled by means of death, so also God's grace rules by means of righteousness, leading us to eternal life through Jesus Christ our Lord.

Chapter 6

Dead to Sin but Alive in Union with Christ

1What shall we say, then? Should we continue to live in sin so that God's grace will increase?

2Certainly not! We have died to sin — how then can we go on living in it?

3 For surely you know that when we were baptized into union with Christ Jesus, we were baptized into union with his death.

4 By our baptism, then, we were buried with him and shared his death, in order that, just as Christ was raised from death by the glorious power of the Father, so also we might live a new life.

5 For since we have become one with him in dying as he did, in the same way we shall be one with him by being raised to life as he was.

6 And we know that our old being has been put to death with Christ on his cross, in order that the power of the sinful self might be destroyed, so that we should no longer be the slaves of sin.

7 For when people die, they are set free from the power of sin.

"So that we should no longer be the slaves of sin" (6.6)

8 Since we have died with Christ, we believe that we will also live with him.

9 For we know that Christ has been raised from death and will never die again — death will no longer rule over him.

10 And so, because he died, sin has no power over him; and now he lives his life in fellowship with God.

11 In the same way you are to think of yourselves as dead, so far as sin is concerned, but living in fellowship with God through Christ Jesus.

12 Sin must no longer rule in your mortal bodies, so that you obey the desires of your natural self.

13 Nor must you surrender any part of yourselves to sin to be used for wicked purposes. Instead, give yourselves to God, as those who have been brought from death to life, and surrender your whole being to him to be used for righteous purposes.

14 Sin must not be your master; for you do not live under law but under God's grace.

Slaves of Righteousness

15 What, then? Shall we sin, because we are not under law but under God's grace? By no means!

16 Surely you know that when you surrender yourselves as slaves to obey someone, you are in fact the slaves of the master you obey — either of sin, which results in death, or of obedience, which results in being put right with God.

17 But thanks be to God! For though at one time you were slaves to sin, you have obeyed with all your heart the truths found in the teaching you received.

18 You were set free from sin and became the slaves of righteousness.

19 (I use everyday language because of the weakness of your natural selves.) At one time you surrendered yourselves entirely as slaves to impurity and wickedness for wicked purposes. In the same way you must now surrender yourselves entirely as slaves of righteousness for holy purposes.

20 When you were the slaves of sin, you were free from righteousness.

21 What did you gain from doing the things that you are now ashamed of? The result of those things is death!

22 But now you have been set free from sin and are the slaves of God. Your gain is a life fully dedicated to him, and the result is eternal life.

23 For sin pays its wage — death; but God's free gift is eternal life in union with Christ Jesus our Lord.

Chapter 7

An Illustration from Marriage

1 Certainly you will understand what I am about to say, my brothers and sisters, because all of you know about law. The law rules over people only as long as they live.

2 A married woman, for example, is bound by the law to her husband as long as he lives; but if he dies, then she is free from the law that bound her to him.

3 So then, if she lives with another man while her husband is alive, she will be called an adulteress; but if her husband dies, she is legally a free woman and does not commit adultery if she marries another man.

4 That is how it is with you, my sisters and brothers. As far as the Law is concerned, you also have died because you are part of the body of Christ; and now you belong to him who was raised from death in order that we might be useful in the service of God.

5 For when we lived according to our human nature, the sinful desires stirred up by the Law were at work in our bodies, and all we did ended in death.

6 Now, however, we are free from the Law, because we died to that which once held us prisoners. No longer do we serve in the old way of a written law, but in the new way of the Spirit.

Law and Sin

7 Shall we say, then, that the Law itself is sinful? Of course not! But it was the Law that made me know what sin is. If the Law had not said, "Do not desire what belongs to someone else," I would not have known such a desire.

8 But by means of that commandment sin found its chance to stir up all kinds of selfish desires in me. Apart from law, sin is a dead thing.

⁹I myself was once alive apart from law; but when the commandment came, sin sprang to life, ¹⁰and I died. And the commandment which was meant to bring life, in my case brought death.

¹¹Sin found its chance, and by means of the commandment it deceived me and killed me.

¹²So then, the Law itself is holy, and the commandment is holy, right, and good.

¹³But does this mean that what is good caused my death? By no means! It was sin that did it; by using what is good, sin brought death to me, in order that its true nature as sin might be revealed. And so, by means of the commandment sin is shown to be even more terribly sinful.

The Conflict within Us

¹⁴We know that the Law is spiritual; but I am unspiritual, sold as a slave to sin.

¹⁵I do not understand what I do; for I don't do what I would like to do, but instead I do what I hate.

¹⁶Since what I do is what I don't want to do, this shows that I agree that the Law is right.

¹⁷So I am not really the one who does this thing; rather it is the sin that lives in me.

¹⁸I know that good does not live in me — that is, in my human nature. For even though the desire to do good is in me, I am not able to do it.

19 I don't do the good I want to do; instead, I do the evil that I do not want to do.

20 If I do what I don't want to do, this means that I am no longer the one who does it; instead, it is the sin that lives in me.

21 So I find that this law is at work: when I want to do what is good, what is evil is the only choice I have.

22 My inner being delights in the law of God.

23 But I see a different law at work in my body — a law that fights against the law which my mind approves of. It makes me a prisoner to the law of sin which is at work in my body.

24 What an unhappy man I am! Who will rescue me from this body that is taking me to death?

25 Thanks be to God, who does this through our Lord Jesus Christ!

This, then, is my condition: on my own I can serve God's law only with my mind, while my human nature serves the law of sin.

Chapter 8

Life in the Spirit

1 There is no condemnation now for those who live in union with Christ Jesus.

² For the law of the Spirit, which brings us life in union with Christ Jesus, has set me*i* free from the law of sin and death.

³ What the Law could not do, because human nature was weak, God did. He condemned sin in human nature by sending his own Son, who came with a nature like sinful human nature, to do away with sin.

⁴ God did this so that the righteous demands of the Law might be fully satisfied in us who live according to the Spirit, and not according to human nature.

⁵ Those who live as their human nature tells them to, have their minds controlled by what human nature wants. Those who live as the Spirit tells them to, have their minds controlled by what the Spirit wants.

⁶ To be controlled by human nature results in death; to be controlled by the Spirit results in life and peace.

⁷ And so people become enemies of God when they are controlled by their human nature; for they do not obey God's law, and in fact they cannot obey it.

⁸ Those who obey their human nature cannot please God.

⁹ But you do not live as your human nature tells you to; instead, you live as the Spirit tells you to — if, in fact, God's Spirit lives in you. Whoever does not have the Spirit of Christ does not belong to him.

---

i me; some manuscripts have *you*; others have *us*.

10 But if Christ lives in you, the Spirit is life for you*j* because you have been put right with God, even though your bodies are going to die because of sin.

11 If the Spirit of God, who raised Jesus from death, lives in you, then he who raised Christ from death will also give life to your mortal bodies by the presence of his Spirit in you.

12 So then, my brothers and sisters, we have an obligation, but it is not to live as our human nature wants us to.

13 For if you live according to your human nature, you are going to die; but if by the Spirit you put to death your sinful actions, you will live.

14 Those who are led by God's Spirit are God's children.

15 For the Spirit that God has given you does not make you slaves and cause you to be afraid; instead, the Spirit makes you God's children, and by the Spirit's power we cry out to God, "Father! my Father!"

16 God's Spirit joins himself to our spirits to declare that we are God's children.

17 Since we are his children, we will possess the blessings he keeps for his people, and we will also possess with Christ what God has kept for him; for if we share Christ's suffering, we will also share his glory.

---

j the Spirit is life for you; or your spirit is alive.

The Future Glory

[18] I consider that what we suffer at this present time cannot be compared at all with the glory that is going to be revealed to us.

[19] All of creation waits with eager longing for God to reveal his children.

[20] For creation was condemned to lose its purpose, not of its own will, but because God willed it to be so. Yet there was the hope [21] that creation itself would one day be set free from its slavery to decay and would share the glorious freedom of the children of God.

[22] For we know that up to the present time all of creation groans with pain, like the pain of childbirth.

[23] But it is not just creation alone which groans; we who have the Spirit as the first of God's gifts also groan within ourselves, as we wait for God to make us his children and[k] set our whole being free.

[24] For it was by hope that we were saved; but if we see what we hope for, then it is not really hope. For which of us hopes for something we see?

[25] But if we hope for what we do not see, we wait for it with patience.

[26] In the same way the Spirit also comes to help us, weak as we are. For we do not know how we ought to pray; the

---

k Some manuscripts do not have *make us his children and*.

Spirit himself pleads with God for us in groans that words cannot express.

27 And God, who sees into our hearts, knows what the thought of the Spirit is; because the Spirit pleads with God on behalf of his people and in accordance with his will.

28 We know that in all things God works for good with those who love him,*I* those whom he has called according to his purpose.

29 Those whom God had already chosen he also set apart to become like his Son, so that the Son would be the eldest brother in a large family.

30 And so those whom God set apart, he called; and those he called, he put right with himself, and he shared his glory with them.

God's Love in Christ Jesus

31 In view of all this, what can we say? If God is for us, who can be against us?

32 Certainly not God, who did not even keep back his own Son, but offered him for us all! He gave us his Son — will he not also freely give us all things?

33 Who will accuse God's chosen people? God himself declares them not guilty!

I *in all things God works for good with those who love him;* some manuscripts have *all things work for good for those who love God.*

34 Who, then, will condemn them? Not Christ Jesus, who died, or rather, who was raised to life and is at the right-hand side of God, pleading with him for us!

35 Who, then, can separate us from the love of Christ? Can trouble do it, or hardship or persecution or hunger or poverty or danger or death?

36 As the scripture says,

> "For your sake we are in danger of death at all times;
> we are treated like sheep that are going to be
> slaughtered."

37 No, in all these things we have complete victory through him who loved us!

38 For I am certain that nothing can separate us from his love: neither death nor life, neither angels nor other heavenly rulers or powers, neither the present nor the future, 39 neither the world above nor the world below — there is nothing in all creation that will ever be able to separate us from the love of God which is ours through Christ Jesus our Lord.

Chapter 9

God and his People

1 I am speaking the truth; I belong to Christ and I do not lie. My conscience, ruled by the Holy Spirit, also assures me that I am not lying 2 when I say how great is my sorrow, how

endless the pain in my heart ³for my people, my own flesh and blood! For their sake I could wish that I myself were under God's curse and separated from Christ.

⁴They are God's people; he made them his children and revealed his glory to them; he made his covenants[m] with them and gave them the Law; they have the true worship; they have received God's promises; ⁵they are descended from the famous Hebrew ancestors; and Christ, as a human being, belongs to their race. May God, who rules over all, be praised for ever![n] Amen.

⁶I am not saying that the promise of God has failed; for not all the people of Israel are the people of God.

⁷Nor are all Abraham's descendants the children of God. God said to Abraham, "It is through Isaac that you will have the descendants I promised you."

⁸This means that the children born in the usual way[o] are not the children of God; instead, the children born as a result of God's promise are regarded as the true descendants.

⁹For God's promise was made in these words: "At the right time[p] I will come back, and Sarah will have a son."

---

[m] *covenants*; some manuscripts have *covenant.*
[n] *May God, who rules over all, be praised for ever!*; or *And may he, who is God ruling over all, be praised for ever!*
[o] *children born in the usual way*: This refers to the descendants Abraham had through Ishmael, his son by Hagar (see Gal 4.22–23).
[p] *At the right time*; or *At this time next year.*

10 And this is not all. For Rebecca's two sons had the same father, our ancestor Isaac.

11-12 But in order that the choice of one son might be completely the result of God's own purpose, God said to her, "The elder will serve the younger." He said this before they were born, before they had done anything either good or bad; so God's choice was based on his call, and not on anything they had done.

13 As the scripture says, "I loved Jacob, but I hated Esau."

14 Shall we say, then, that God is unjust? Not at all.

15 For he said to Moses, "I will have mercy on anyone I wish; I will take pity on anyone I wish."

16 So then, everything depends, not on what human beings want or do, but only on God's mercy.

17 For the scripture says to the king of Egypt, "I made you king in order to use you to show my power and to spread my fame over the whole world."

18 So then, God has mercy on anyone he wishes, and he makes stubborn anyone he wishes.

God's Anger and Mercy

19 But one of you will say to me, "If this is so, how can God find fault with anyone? Who can resist God's will?"

20 But who are you, my friend, to answer God back? A clay pot does not ask the man who made it, "Why did you make me like this?"

21 After all, the man who makes the pots has the right to use the clay as he wishes, and to make two pots from the same lump of clay, one for special occasions and the other for ordinary use.

22 And the same is true of what God has done. He wanted to show his anger and to make his power known. But he was very patient in enduring those who were the objects of his anger, who were doomed to destruction.

23 And he also wanted to reveal his abundant glory, which was poured out on us who are the objects of his mercy, those of us whom he has prepared to receive his glory.

24 For we are the people he called, not only from among the Jews but also from among the Gentiles.

25 This is what he says in the book of Hosea:

"The people who were not mine
    I will call 'My People'.
The nation that I did not love
    I will call 'My Beloved'.
26 And in the very place where they were told, 'You are
        not my people,'
        there they will be called the children of the living
        God."

27 And Isaiah exclaims about Israel: "Even if the people of Israel are as many as the grains of sand by the sea, yet only a few of them will be saved; 28 for the Lord will quickly settle his full account with the world."

29 It is as Isaiah had said before, "If the Lord Almighty had not left us some descendants, we would have become like Sodom, we would have been like Gomorrah."

Paul's Prayer for Israel

30 So we say that the Gentiles, who were not trying to put themselves right with God, were put right with him through faith; 31 while God's people, who were seeking a law that would put them right with God, did not find it.

32 And why not? Because they did not depend on faith but on what they did. And so they stumbled over the "stumbling stone" 33 that the scripture speaks of:

"Look, I place in Zion a stone
that will make people stumble,
a rock that will make them fall.
But whoever believes in him will not be disappointed."

Chapter 10

1 My brothers and sisters, how I wish with all my heart that my own people might be saved! How I pray to God for them!

2 I can assure you that they are deeply devoted to God; but their devotion is not based on true knowledge.

3 They have not known the way in which God puts people right with himself, and instead, they have tried to set up their own way; and so they did not submit themselves to God's way of putting people right.

4 For Christ has brought the Law to an end, so that everyone who believes is put right with God.

Salvation is for All

5 Moses wrote this about being put right with God by obeying the Law: "Whoever obeys the commands of the Law will live."

6 But what the scripture says about being put right with God through faith is this: "You are not to ask yourself, Who will go up into heaven?" (that is, to bring Christ down).

7 "Nor are you to ask, Who will go down into the world below?" (that is, to bring Christ up from death).

8 What it says is this: "God's message is near you, on your lips and in your heart" — that is, the message of faith that we preach.

9 If you confess that Jesus is Lord and believe that God raised him from death, you will be saved.

10 For it is by our faith that we are put right with God; it is by our confession that we are saved.

11 The scripture says, "Whoever believes in him will not be disappointed."

12 This includes everyone, because there is no difference between Jews and Gentiles; God is the same Lord of all and richly blesses all who call to him.

13 As the scripture says, "Everyone who calls out to the Lord for help will be saved."

14 But how can they call to him for help if they have not believed? And how can they believe if they have not heard the message? And how can they hear if the message is not proclaimed?

15 And how can the message be proclaimed if the messengers are not sent out? As the scripture says, "How wonderful is the coming of messengers who bring good news!"

16 But not all have accepted the Good News. Isaiah himself said, "Lord, who believed our message?"

17 So then, faith comes from hearing the message, and the message comes through preaching Christ.

18 But I ask: is it true that they did not hear the message? Of course they did — for as the scripture says:

"The sound of their voice went out to all the world;
     their words reached the ends of the earth."

19 Again I ask: did the people of Israel not understand? Moses himself is the first one to answer:

"I will use a so-called nation
     to make my people jealous;
and by means of a nation of fools
     I will make my people angry."

20 And Isaiah is even bolder when he says,

"I was found by those who were not looking for me;
     I appeared to those who were not asking for me."

21 But concerning Israel he says, "All day long I held out my hands to welcome a disobedient and rebellious people."

Chapter 11

God's Mercy on Israel

1 I ask, then: did God reject his own people? Certainly not! I myself am an Israelite, a descendant of Abraham, a member of the tribe of Benjamin.

2 God has not rejected his people, whom he chose from the beginning. You know what the scripture says in the passage where Elijah pleads with God against Israel: 3 "Lord, they have killed your prophets and torn down your altars; I am the only one left, and they are trying to kill me."

4 What answer did God give him? "I have kept for myself 7,000 men who have not worshipped the false god Baal."

5 It is the same way now: there is a small number left of those whom God has chosen because of his grace.

6 His choice is based on his grace, not on what they have done. For if God's choice were based on what people do, then his grace would not be real grace.

7 What then? The people of Israel did not find what they were looking for. It was only the small group that God chose who found it; the rest grew deaf to God's call.

8 As the scripture says, "God made their minds and hearts dull; to this very day they cannot see or hear."

9 And David says:

"May they be caught and trapped at their feasts;
    may they fall, may they be punished!
10 May their eyes be blinded so that they cannot see;
        and make them bend under their troubles at all
            times."

11 I ask, then: when the Jews stumbled, did they fall to their ruin? By no means! Because they sinned, salvation has come to the Gentiles, to make the Jews jealous of them.

12 The sin of the Jews brought rich blessings to the world, and their spiritual poverty brought rich blessings to the Gentiles. Then, how much greater the blessings will be when the complete number of Jews is included!

The Salvation of the Gentiles

13 I am speaking now to you Gentiles: as long as I am an apostle to the Gentiles, I will take pride in my work.

14 Perhaps I can make the people of my own race jealous, and so be able to save some of them.

15 For when they were rejected, the human race was changed from God's enemies into his friends. What will it be, then, when they are accepted? It will be life for the dead!

16 If the first piece of bread is given to God, then the whole loaf is his also; and if the roots of a tree are offered to God, the branches are his also.

17 Some of the branches of the cultivated olive tree have been broken off, and a branch of a wild olive tree has been joined to it. You Gentiles are like that wild olive tree, and now you share the strong spiritual life of the Jews.

18 So then, you must not despise those who were broken off like branches. How can you be proud? You are just a branch; you don't support the roots — the roots support you.

19 But you will say, "Yes, but the branches were broken off to make room for me."

20 That is true. They were broken off because they did not believe, while you remain in place because you do believe. But do not be proud of it; instead, be afraid.

21 God did not spare the Jews, who are like natural branches; do you think he will spare you?

22 Here we see how kind and how severe God is. He is severe towards those who have fallen, but kind to you — if you continue in his kindness. But if you do not, you too will be broken off.

23 And if the Jews abandon their unbelief, they will be put back in the place where they were; for God is able to do that.

24 You Gentiles are like the branch of a wild olive tree that is broken off and then, contrary to nature, is joined to

a cultivated olive tree. The Jews are like this cultivated tree; and it will be much easier for God to join these broken-off branches to their own tree again.

God's Mercy on All

25 There is a secret truth, my brothers and sisters, which I want you to know, for it will keep you from thinking how wise you are. It is that the stubbornness of the people of Israel is not permanent, but will last only until the complete number of Gentiles comes to God.

26 And this is how all Israel will be saved. As the scripture says:

"The Saviour will come from Zion
    and remove all wickedness from the descendants of
        Jacob.
27I will make this covenant with them
    when I take away their sins."

28 Because they reject the Good News, the Jews are God's enemies for the sake of you Gentiles. But because of God's choice, they are his friends because of their ancestors.

29For God does not change his mind about whom he chooses and blesses.

30 As for you Gentiles, you disobeyed God in the past; but now you have received God's mercy because the Jews were disobedient.

31 In the same way, because of the mercy that you have received, the Jews now disobey God, in order that they also may now[q] receive God's mercy.

32 For God has made all people prisoners of disobedience, so that he might show mercy to them all.

Praise to God

33 How great are God's riches! How deep are his wisdom and knowledge! Who can explain his decisions? Who can understand his ways?

34 As the scripture says:

> "Who knows the mind of the Lord?
>> Who is able to give him advice?
> 35 Who has ever given him anything,
>> so that he had to pay it back?"

36 For all things were created by him, and all things exist through him and for him. To God be the glory for ever! Amen.

Chapter 12

Life in God's Service

1 So then, my brothers and sisters, because of God's great mercy to us I appeal to you: offer yourselves as a living

---

[q] Some manuscripts do not have *now*.

sacrifice to God, dedicated to his service and pleasing to him. This is the true worship that you should offer.

2 Do not conform yourselves to the standards of this world, but let God transform you inwardly by a complete change of your mind. Then you will be able to know the will of God — what is good and is pleasing to him and is perfect.

3 And because of God's gracious gift to me I say to every one of you: do not think of yourself more highly than you should. Instead, be modest in your thinking, and judge yourself according to the amount of faith that God has given you.

4 We have many parts in the one body, and all these parts have different functions.

5 In the same way, though we are many, we are one body in union with Christ, and we are all joined to each other as different parts of one body.

6 So we are to use our different gifts in accordance with the grace that God has given us. If our gift is to speak God's message, we should do it according to the faith that we have; 7 if it is to serve, we should serve; if it is to teach, we should teach; 8 if it is to encourage others, we should do so. Whoever shares with others should do it generously; whoever has authority should work hard; whoever shows kindness to others should do it cheerfully.

9 Love must be completely sincere. Hate what is evil, hold on to what is good.

10 Love one another warmly as Christian brothers and sisters, and be eager to show respect for one another.

11 Work hard and do not be lazy. Serve the Lord with a heart full of devotion.

12 Let your hope keep you joyful, be patient in your troubles, and pray at all times.

13 Share your belongings with your needy fellow-Christians, and open your homes to strangers.

14 Ask God to bless those who persecute you — yes, ask him to bless, not to curse.

15 Be happy with those who are happy, weep with those who weep.

16 Have the same concern for everyone. Do not be proud, but accept humble duties.*r* Do not think of yourselves as wise.

17 If someone has done you wrong, do not repay him with a wrong. Try to do what everyone considers to be good.

18 Do everything possible on your part to live in peace with everybody.

19 Never take revenge, my friends, but instead let God's anger do it. For the scripture says, "I will take revenge, I will pay back, says the Lord."

20 Instead, as the scripture says: "If your enemies are hungry, feed them; if they are thirsty, give them a drink; for by doing this you will make them burn with shame."

---

r accept humble duties; or make friends with humble people.

21 Do not let evil defeat you; instead, conquer evil with good.

Chapter 13

Duties towards the State Authorities

1 Everyone must obey the state authorities, because no authority exists without God's permission, and the existing authorities have been put there by God.

2 Whoever opposes the existing authority opposes what God has ordered; and anyone who does so will bring judgement on himself.

3 For rulers are not to be feared by those who do good, but by those who do evil. Would you like to be unafraid of those in authority? Then do what is good, and they will praise you, 4 because they are God's servants working for your own good. But if you do evil, then be afraid of them, because their power to punish is real. They are God's servants and carry out God's punishment on those who do evil.

5 For this reason you must obey the authorities — not just because of God's punishment, but also as a matter of conscience.

6 That is also why you pay taxes, because the authorities are working for God when they fulfil their duties.

7Pay, then, what you owe them; pay them your personal and property taxes, and show respect and honour for them all.

Duties towards One Another

8 Be under obligation to no one — the only obligation you have is to love one another. Whoever does this has obeyed the Law.

9The commandments, "Do not commit adultery; do not commit murder; do not steal; do not desire what belongs to someone else" — all these, and any others besides, are summed up in the one command, "Love your neighbour as you love yourself."

10 If you love someone, you will never do them wrong; to love, then, is to obey the whole Law.

11 You must do this, because you know that the time has come for you to wake up from your sleep. For the moment when we will be saved is closer now than it was when we first believed.

12 The night is nearly over, day is almost here. Let us stop doing the things that belong to the dark, and let us take up weapons for fighting in the light.

13 Let us conduct ourselves properly, as people who live in the light of day — no orgies or drunkenness, no immorality or indecency, no fighting or jealousy.

14 But take up the weapons of the Lord Jesus Christ, and stop paying attention to your sinful nature and satisfying its desires.

Chapter 14

Do not Judge One Another

1 Welcome those who are weak in faith, but do not argue with them about their personal opinions.

2 Some people's faith allows them to eat anything, but the person who is weak in the faith eats only vegetables.

3 Those who will eat anything are not to despise those who don't; while those who eat only vegetables are not to pass judgement on those who will eat anything; for God has accepted them.

4 Who are you to judge someone else's servants? It is their own Master who will decide whether they succeed or fail. And they will succeed, because the Lord is able to make them succeed.

5 Some people think that a certain day is more important than other days, while others think that all days are the same. We should each firmly make up our own minds.

6 Those who think highly of a certain day do so in honour of the Lord; those who will eat anything do so in honour of the Lord, because they give thanks to God for the food. Those who refuse to eat certain things do so in honour of the Lord, and they give thanks to God.

7None of us lives for himself only, none of us dies for himself only.

8If we live, it is for the Lord that we live, and if we die, it is for the Lord that we die. So whether we live or die, we belong to the Lord.

9For Christ died and rose to life in order to be the Lord of the living and of the dead.

10You then, who eat only vegetables — why do you pass judgement on others? And you who eat anything — why do you despise other believers? All of us will stand before God to be judged by him.

11For the scripture says:

"As surely as I am the living God, says the Lord,
　everyone will kneel before me,
　and everyone will confess that I am God."

12Every one of us, then, will have to give an account of ourselves to God.

Do not Make One Another Fall

13So then, let us stop judging one another. Instead, you should decide never to do anything that would make another stumble or fall into sin.

14My union with the Lord Jesus makes me certain that no food is of itself ritually unclean; but if a person believes that some food is unclean, then it becomes unclean for that person.

15 If you hurt your brother or sister because of something you eat, then you are no longer acting from love. Do not let the food that you eat ruin the person for whom Christ died!

16 Do not let what you regard as good get a bad name.

17 For God's Kingdom is not a matter of eating and drinking, but of the righteousness, peace, and joy which the Holy Spirit gives.

18 And when people serve Christ in this way, they please God and are approved by others.

19 So then, we must always aim**s** at those things that bring peace and that help to strengthen one another.

20 Do not, because of food, destroy what God has done. All foods may be eaten, but it is wrong to eat anything that will cause someone else to fall into sin.

21 The right thing to do is to keep from eating meat, drinking wine, or doing anything else that will make your brother or sister fall.

22 Keep what you believe about this matter, then, between yourself and God.

"Help the weak" (15.1)

---

s *we must always aim*; some manuscripts have *we always aim*.

Happy are those who do not feel guilty when they do something they judge is right!

23 But if they have doubts about what they eat, God condemns them when they eat it, because their action is not based on faith. And anything that is not based on faith is sin.

Chapter 15

Please Others, not Yourselves

1 We who are strong in the faith ought to help the weak to carry their burdens. We should not please ourselves.

2 Instead, we should all please our brothers and sisters for their own good, in order to build them up in the faith.

3 For Christ did not please himself. Instead, as the scripture says, "The insults which are hurled at you have fallen on me."

4 Everything written in the Scriptures was written to teach us, in order that we might have hope through the patience and encouragement which the Scriptures give us.

5 And may God, the source of patience and encouragement, enable you to have the same point of view among yourselves by following the example of Christ Jesus, 6 so that all of you together may praise with one voice the God and Father of our Lord Jesus Christ.

Good News for the Gentiles

7 Accept one another, then, for the glory of God, as Christ has accepted you.

8 For I tell you that Christ's life of service was on behalf of the Jews, to show that God is faithful, to make his promises to their ancestors come true, 9 and to enable even the Gentiles to praise God for his mercy. As the scripture says:

"And so I will praise you among the Gentiles;
I will sing praises to you."

10 Again it says,

"Rejoice, Gentiles, with God's people!"

11 And again,

"Praise the Lord, all Gentiles;
praise him, all peoples!"

12 And again, Isaiah says,

"A descendant of Jesse will appear;
he will come to rule the Gentiles,
and they will put their hope in him."

13 May God, the source of hope, fill you with all joy and peace by means of your faith in him, so that your hope will continue to grow by the power of the Holy Spirit.

Paul's Reason for Writing so Boldly

14 My brothers and sisters, I myself feel sure that you are full of goodness, that you have all knowledge, and that you are able to teach one another.

15 But in this letter I have been quite bold about certain subjects of which I have reminded you. I have been bold because of the privilege God has given me 16 of being a servant of Christ Jesus to work for the Gentiles. I serve like a priest in preaching the Good News from God, in order that the Gentiles may be an offering acceptable to God, dedicated to him by the Holy Spirit.

17 In union with Christ Jesus, then, I can be proud of my service for God.

18 I will be bold and speak only about what Christ has done through me to lead the Gentiles to obey God. He has done this by means of words and deeds, 19 by the power of miracles and wonders, and by the power of the Spirit of God. And so, in travelling all the way from Jerusalem to Illyricum, I have proclaimed fully the Good News about Christ.

20 My ambition has always been to proclaim the Good News in places where Christ has not been heard of, so as not to build on a foundation laid by someone else.

21 As the scripture says:

"Those who were not told about him will see,
and those who have not heard will understand."

Paul's Plan to Visit Rome

22 And so I have been prevented many times from coming to you.

23 But now that I have finished my work in these regions and since I have been wanting for so many years to come to see you, 24 I hope to do so now. I would like to see you on my way to Spain, and be helped by you to go there, after I have enjoyed visiting you for a while.

25 Just now, however, I am going to Jerusalem in the service of God's people there.

26 For the churches in Macedonia and Achaia have freely decided to give an offering to help the poor among God's people in Jerusalem.

27 That decision was their own; but, as a matter of fact, they have an obligation to help them. Since the Jews shared their spiritual blessings with the Gentiles, the Gentiles ought to use their material blessings to help the Jews.

28 When I have finished this task and have handed over to them all the money that has been raised for them, I shall leave for Spain and visit you on my way there.

29 When I come to you, I know that I shall come with a full measure of the blessing of Christ.

30 I urge you, brothers and sisters, by our Lord Jesus Christ and by the love that the Spirit gives: join me in praying fervently to God for me.

31 Pray that I may be kept safe from the unbelievers in Judea and that my service in Jerusalem may be acceptable to God's people there.

32 And so I will come to you full of joy, if it is God's will, and enjoy a refreshing visit to you.

33 May God, our source of peace, be with all of you. Amen.

Chapter 16

Personal Greetings

1 I recommend to you our sister Phoebe, who serves the church at Cenchreae.

2 Receive her in the Lord's name, as God's people should, and give her any help she may need from you; for she herself has been a good friend to many people and also to me.

3 I send greetings to Priscilla and Aquila, my fellow-workers in the service of Christ Jesus; 4 they risked their lives for me. I am grateful to them — not only I, but all the Gentile churches as well.

5 Greetings also to the church that meets in their house.

Greetings to my dear friend Epaenetus, who was the first in the province of Asia to believe in Christ.

6 Greetings to Mary, who has worked so hard for you.

7Greetings also to Andronicus and Junia,*t* fellow-Jews who were in prison with me; they are well known among the apostles, and they became Christians before I did.

8 My greetings to Ampliatus, my dear friend in the fellowship of the Lord.

9Greetings also to Urbanus, our fellow-worker in Christ's service, and to Stachys, my dear friend.

10 Greetings to Apelles, whose loyalty to Christ has been proved. Greetings to those who belong to the family of Aristobulus.

11Greetings to Herodion, a fellow-Jew, and to the Christians in the family of Narcissus.

12 My greetings to Tryphaena and Tryphosa, who work in the Lord's service, and to my dear friend Persis, who has done so much work for the Lord.

13I send greetings to Rufus, that outstanding worker in the Lord's service, and to his mother, who has always treated me like a son.

14 My greetings to Asyncritus, Phlegon, Hermes, Patrobas, Hermas, and all the other Christian brothers and sisters with them.

15Greetings to Philologus and Julia, to Nereus and his sister, to Olympas and to all of God's people who are with them.

---

t *Junia;* or *Junias;* some manuscripts have *Julia.*

16 Greet one another with a holy kiss. All the churches of Christ send you their greetings.

Final Instructions

17 I urge you, my brothers and sisters: watch out for those who cause divisions and upset people's faith and go against the teaching which you have received. Keep away from them!

18 For those who do such things are not serving Christ our Lord, but their own appetites. By their fine words and flattering speech they deceive innocent people.

19 Everyone has heard of your loyalty to the gospel, and for this reason I am happy about you. I want you to be wise about what is good, but innocent in what is evil.

20 And God, our source of peace, will soon crush Satan under your feet.

The grace of our Lord Jesus be with you.[u]

21 Timothy, my fellow-worker, sends you his greetings; and so do Lucius, Jason, and Sosipater, fellow-Jews.

22 I, Tertius, the writer of this letter, send you Christian greetings.

23 My host Gaius, in whose house the church meets, sends you his greetings; Erastus, the city treasurer, and our brother Quartus send you their greetings.[v]

[u] Some manuscripts omit this sentence.
[v] Some manuscripts add verse 24: *The grace of our Lord Jesus Christ be with you all. Amen*; others add this after verse 27.

Concluding Prayer of Praise

25 Let us give glory to God! He is able to make you stand firm in your faith, according to the Good News I preach about Jesus Christ and according to the revelation of the secret truth which was hidden for long ages in the past.

26 Now, however, that truth has been brought out into the open through the writings of the prophets; and by the command of the eternal God it is made known to all nations, so that all may believe and obey.

27 To the only God, who alone is all-wise, be glory through Jesus Christ for ever! Amen.**w**

w Some manuscripts have verses 25–27 here and after 14.23; others have them only after 14.23; one has them after 15.33.

Where to find ...